SPEECH

OF

MR. EWING, OF OHIO,

ON

MR. BRADBURY'S RESOLUTIONS.

DELIVERED IN THE SENATE OF THE UNITED STATES, TUESDAY, JANUARY 7, 1851.

WASHINGTON:
GIDEON & CO., PRINTERS.
1851.

SPEECH

OF

MR. EWING, OF OHIO,

ON

MR. BRADBURY'S RESOLUTIONS.

DELIVERED IN THE SENATE OF THE UNITED STATES, TUESDAY, JANUARY 7, 1851.

WASHINGTON:
GIDEON & CO., PRINTERS.
1851.

SPEECH

In Senate, Tuesday, January 7, 1851.

The Senate having resumed the consideration of the resolution in relation to removals from office—

Mr. EWING said:

I expressed my entire willingness on Thursday last, after listening to the remarks of the Senator from Indiana, (Mr. Bright,) to join the issue tendered by gentlemen on the other side. And as it is impossible to adduce all the cases of removal, and to give all the reasons in all the cases, I was willing to take the two prominent cases selected by those gentlemen, and selected with very great care and caution, and to let them stand as the test cases. On my part, in behalf of the late Administration, I was willing, and am still willing, to admit, that if these removals, or if either one of them was wrong, that all were wrong; and I expect a like candid admission on their side, that if those which they have selected as the test cases were right, that all were right; and that they will give up the contest, if the position which they have taken as to these their selected cases cannot be sustained. Gentlemen made their selection after the lapse of much time, and evidently upon much consultation. I infer the fact from their obvious accord in thrusting Gen. Lane and Col. Weller prominently forward as the specially wronged and persecuted victims; from the prompt and general rally at the instant to their defence; from the harmonious agreement of many voices in denouncing these especially as cases of mere naked proscription; and, finally, from the general concurrence of Senators in alleging, by way of aggravation, that the gentlemen thus removed were at the time on the Pacific coast. I do not know that this was the result of a caucus, but there was a wondrous agreement in the assumption of fact and its presentation in argument.

By mutual agreement, then, we will take these cases, chosen by gentlemen on the other side. We will take them with all their circumstances of aggravation, and if I cannot prove that their removals were right and proper, nay, a necessary duty on the part of the late President, then I will agree that he acted upon a wrong principle, and that his removals generally were wrong. If I prove that these were right, then I claim from the other side the admission that his removals were generally right.

These selections are well and judiciously and fairly made. They belong each to his own separate class of officeholders; Col. Weller to those who were wholly unfit for the offices to which they were appointed, incapable of discharging the duties, and unfit to be trusted with the funds necessary for their execution. Gen. Lane belonged to a different class, that of electioneering officeholders, whose violence and abuse and calumny during the Presidential canvass had been such that Gen. Taylor, when he became President, could not, without sacrificing all self-respect, without sacrificing all respect for his political friends, suffer them to remain in office; nay, it was such that, had they had a proper sense of what was due to official propriety, they would of themselves have instantly resigned their offices upon the election of General Taylor, and refused to hold office under a man whom they had so depreciated and calumniated. There is, then, a peculiar fitness in the selection which gentlemen have made. We may test a large number of cases from these two, of which they may be considered the representatives.

I had something to say with respect to Col. Weller a few days ago, and it is not necessary that I should now repeat what I then said, nor refer to the documents to which I then referred. I will merely add two particulars, to which I did not deem it necessary to refer, but which, as gentlemen are hard to satisfy, the occasion now calls for.

But, before proceeding to the question, I will remark, that I have not sought this controversy, but have shunned it; not, however, in fear of the result, for I knew at the commencement how it must end; but from an unfeigned reluctance to engage in a discussion involving personal character and personal conduct. Hence it is that I have said as little as I could possibly say, without doing injustice to General Taylor's Administration, that would injure the character or wound the feelings of either. If I touch them now with a less gentle hand, they must thank their friends, who persisted in thrusting them in our faces. But, in order to take up the first branch of my subject properly, I must refer to the debate of the 12th of December, in which the Senator from Michigan took a part. That Senator made an inquiry of me during that debate in these words: "But will the honorable Senator tell me that Col. Weller would have been removed if he had been a Whig?"

I replied, in answer to the question of the honorable Senator from Michigan, as follows:

"And I can say to the honorable Senator from Michigan, (Mr. Cass,) in reply to his inquiry, that had Col. Weller been a Whig, and had my information concerning him been what it was and from the same reliable sources, I would have unhesitatingly advised his removal."

I had hoped that my reply would have been perfectly satisfactory to the Senator, and especially after the remarks made by me the other day.

Mr. Cass. If the Senator from Ohio will allow me, I will state that my inquiry was in allusion to the ground of removal which he had then stated, which was with respect to the accounts of Col. Weller. He had not then referred to the character of Col. Weller, and my remark had no reference to that.

Mr. Ewing. I hoped that the Senator would have been satisfied with my reply, knowing, as I was convinced he did, that there were other charges of grave import against Col. Weller, and knowing also, as I supposed he did, that I withheld them from an unwillingness, unless absolutely compelled by the force of circumstances, to speak here of the defects and vices of men. But when next the Senator spoke, he saw fit to consider me as having stated specifically all I knew of Col. Weller, and all the facts which influenced the President to remove him; and, giving me credit for good intentions, he expressed himself incredulous of my assertion, that I would have advised the removal of Colonel Weller had he been a Whig. And in these remarks the Senator from Michigan took particular pains to confine the issue to what I never made an issue, which was, whether Colonel Weller was removed under and by the operations of a particular act of Congress. Well, I agree that he was not. I never said that he was, nor intimated any such thing. But the Senator said, when he last addressed the Senate on the subject, that he would not be "driven from his point." That is, the Senator was determined to confine the cause of removal to the operation of that particular law which I did not name, and which had nothing to do with it. I have no issue with the honorable Senator; he took his ground entirely out of my line of march, and it would have been most unreasonable for me to go quite out of my way to drive him from a position which he had a perfect right to occupy, and which interfered not at all with mine.

As the Senator is not satisfied with the evidence already adduced, I will now offer one other item, and hope it will be sufficient. It is a certified copy of the report of a master in chancery, who was appointed by the court of common pleas of Butler county to inquire into the defalcation of Colonel Weller and two other individuals who were entrusted with a public fund belonging to that county. I will read a short extract from that report, premising, however, that all the commissioners were good Democrats, and Mr. McBride, the master in chancery, a Democrat also, and a personal friend of Colonel Weller. The money entrusted to these persons was the part of the surplus fund belonging to that county, a large amount of which Colonel Weller had converted to his own use, and failed to account for. This fact I well knew when Colonel Weller was removed; and the Senator from Michigan must have known that I knew and referred to it when I told him, the other day, that from the facts within my knowledge I would have advised the removal of Colonel Weller had he been a Whig. The extract is as follows:

"The amounts due said funds by other debtors than said defendants, whose notes, bonds, and mortgages have been put into my possession, may be found in tabular statement herewith filed, (marked B,) amounting in all to the sum of $30,733 46, leaving in the hands of the defendants, and to be acccounted for by them, the sum of $24,050 74. Of this sum I find, according to notes and receipts on file, that James H. Ward owes the sum of $4,687 83, (for particulars as to dates and accounts, see his account on file marked C,) and that Lowen R. Cooch, according to similar vouchers and evidence on file, owes of this sum the amount of $2,429 87, received at times and in amounts as specified in his account on file, (marked D,) leaving to be accounted for by John B. Weller, the other defendant, and agent of the commissioners, the sum of $16,933 06. At what time or times, or in what amounts, this sum was received by Mr. Weller, or at what time he became chargeable therewith, I have not been able to ascertain."

Thus it appears, Mr. President, that Colonel Weller was a defaulter to his own county at the time of his appointment in a large amount, and it was a fact known to me at the time of his removal—not then by the certified report of the master, but by undoubted information. And it is proper to add, that he was known to be habitually intemperate. Nobody denies this—nobody doubts it. The duty he was to discharge was exceedingly important, as he had the command of men and the control of a large sum of money. There was placed in his hands, immediately upon his appointment, upwards of $33,000 of the public money. He gave no bond—he was not required to give any. He left the United States with this money while the suit was pending, after the matter was referred to the master, and before his report was made, and he failed to render an account or present a statement to the commissioner, but left him to find out the date and amount of his defalcation as he best could. He sailed for Panama, as I showed the other day, more than a month before the duties of his commission required him, and the only object that I can conjecture he had in view was to be out of the United States before the new Administration should come into power. Certainly he did not forward the business of his commission by going so hastily, for he was further from the place of his destination, in point of time, at the end of the month, at Panama, than he would have been in New York the same day. He could have obtained transportation from New York for himself and his party, while he had provided none, and could obtain none, from Panama. And from the accounts we had of his conduct while lingering there, any one must have been satisfied that he was wholly unfit to be entrusted with the command of men or the expenditure of public money. Now, I say that, had Colonel Weller been a political partisan connected with me, no matter how closely, and had that office been in my department, I should most unhesitatingly have advised his removal, and would have felt it inexcusable to trust so large an amount of the public money in his hands. The Senator from Michigan may be incredulous yet, but I venture to assert that, had it been his own private funds which were in the hands of Colonel Weller, he would have taken them out, if he could get them, immediately. What he would have done with regard to public funds of which he had the care, it is for him and not for me to determine. But I have no doubt that had he occupied the Executive chair he would have removed Colonel Weller from *that* situation, however else he might have bestowed him.

But further to remove doubts from the mind of the Senator from Michigan, I must be permitted to say, that the very case once occurred, that I did remove, or rather advise the removal of a Whig, who was in every way qualified for his office except in the one particular, merely because I had ascertained he was a defaulter in his own State. I advised his removal, and Gen. Taylor removed him. I do not wish to name, nor is it necessary that I should name, the individual. I will, however, inform the Senator from Michigan, privately, of the person and the office, if he desires it.

So much, Mr. President, for Col. Weller. I do not wish to dwell upon his case any longer, or ever return to it again, unless the Senator from Michigan still thinks that my statement and asseveration needs further support. If he does, I will give it to him in public or in private, as he may desire.

Mr. Cass. I will make my statement after you have done.

Mr. Ewing. I will now say one word as to this case of *"naked proscription for opinion's sake;"* for that this removal has been pronounced by a half a dozen voices here. Col. Weller, a Democrat, wholly without qualifications, not trustworthy, not fit for the office, was removed from it, and Col. Frémont, another *Democrat*, most highly qualified, in every respect trustworthy, of perfect fitness and capacity for the duties of the office, was appointed in his place. This is the proscription for opinion's sake so eloquently denounced by gentlemen on the other side of the chamber.

Perhaps I ought to explain one thing further, however, before I leave this case. Col. Weller was, according to well settled usage, clearly *entitled* to an office from the Democratic party. The previous Administrations here had always given the defeated candidate for Governor of Ohio some office under the Federal Government, and of course Col. Weller must have some one. But my point is, and I do not mean to be driven from it, that this was not the proper office. They selected badly—a foreign mission, being the just reward for the services of the candidate, and the usual salvo for his feelings, wounded by defeat.

Before proceeding to the case of Gen. Lane, I will consider for a moment an item of Executive history, kindly furnished to me by the Senator from Indiana. He says:

"I will read a letter which I have in my possession, first premising that, at the time Gen. Lane was Governor of Oregon, the duties of Governors of Territories, Indian agents, and similar officers were under the supervision of the Department of the Interior. There had been somewhat of a conflict between that Department and the Department of State as to which was entitled to the jurisdiction of these officers. I understand that latterly it has been settled in favor of the Department of State, and therefore that became the proper place to which I should apply for information."

Now, this is all new information to me—entirely so. I never heard or suspected that there was the slightest question between those two Departments as to jurisdiction. The Department of State had jurisdiction over the Territorial officers proper. The Department of the Interior over the Superintendent of Indian Affairs. The Governor of Oregon performed the double duty. He was the Governor and was *ex officio* Superintendent of Indian Affairs. His office of Governor was within, and he was appointed and removed through, the State Department. The Department of the Interior had nothing to do with it, except to attend and see to the discharge of his duties as superintendent. Hence it is that everything which related to the Indian affairs came to the Department of the Interior, and all that related to his other duties to the Department of State. I do not know where the Senator got his information—from what letter-writer, or in what newspaper he found it; but he stated it here as a matter of history, of which he had become well informed. There is a great deal of history which gets abroad with just as much foundation as that. Owing to the fact that Gen. Lane was not from my State, and not in my Department, I did not treasure up in my mind the particulars of his removal, the mere passing events of a day, but I remembered in a very general manner his neglect of duty as Superintendent of Indian Affairs, and the complaints made against him in that capacity, and on the spur of the moment I stated them as I remembered them; and I find, on examination, that my memory has not misled me. I said:

"As to Governor Lane, no report was made by him to the Department for a very long time after his appointment. Great complaints were made against him from the Territory of Oregon, and from the most authentic and reliable sources; those which the Executive ought to respect."

As a matter of fact and memory at the moment, I said that this was the case—not that he was removed on this ground; for, having nothing to do with his removal, I could not answer for its cause, any further than I have said. Knowing by whom it was done, I knew it was rightfully done.

Now, with respect to the first of the objections I stated against Governor Lane—namely, that he neglected to report as Superintendent of Indian Affairs—the Senator from Indiana, not now present, (Mr. Bright,) offered as an apology or explanation that Gen. Lane was appointed by telegraphic despatch, and that he immediately set out, making a toilsome journey over an inhospitable region, and did not reach Oregon until January or February. Well, these are all truths; but his first report does not bear date until October, and Gen. Lane knew perfectly well that it was necessary for the Department to receive his report earlier than that, in order to be able to make their report to Congress as to the condition of the Indian tribes in Oregon, and to recommend to that body what was necessary to be done for the benefit of the Indians and of our own people.

Mr. Whitcomb. If the Senator will allow me, I merely wish to state that Governor Lane arrived in Oregon on the 3d of March, if my information is correct.

Mr. Ewing. Very well; I could not remember exactly. He arrived there on the 3d of March, and he made his report in October. Now, he knew perfectly well that the necessities of the Department required that as much information of the actual condition of affairs in Oregon as could be got, should be presented to the Department as early as possible. Had this been an Administration which he was inclined to favor, does any man believe he would have withheld his report till October, when it could not reach the Department till it was too late to have it embraced in the report made to Congress? Was he, in this, prompt and diligent in the discharge of his official duties?

I can give an example of what can be done by an officer who is on speaking terms with the Administration whom he serves. The new Superintendent of Indian Affairs (Mr. Dart) reached Oregon on the 26th of September, and on the 24th of October, twenty-eight days after his arrival, he forwarded to the Department a report, and a very satisfactory one, as far as he could go, and he followed it up with the reports as fast as he had been able to get information. This man is intent on doing his duty.

Now, I felt it to be a great wrong on the part of Gen. Lane, and I felt that the Department wanted a superintendent there who would attend to his duty, and give the information which was desired. The honorable Senator from Indiana said that Gen. Lane had not time to go all over the Territory and find out all about the Indians; that it was a great Territory, and he could not do it in such brief time as I seemed to require. True; but he had time to give the information respecting the Indians so far as they came immediately in contact with the whites, and under his own personal observation—so far, indeed, as to show what was necessary to keep the two races, as far as practicable, separate, and to enable them to get on peaceably with each other. This he could have done within two or three months after reaching Oregon, and he ought to have done it.

The Senator from Indiana says that the law did not require him to make a report at any specified time or times. True, the law does not say that he should make a report within three or five months; and I suppose he stood upon the law, and was disposed to do no more than its strict letter required of him. If so, and if he was right, the office is useless. The law does not and cannot point out the exact duties to be performed in time and manner.

This general fact I mentioned, and I stated it the other day from memory;

and I remembered, too, that there had been complaints against General Lane by individuals from Oregon, who were entitled to credit, which I designated as the most reliable sources. I know that the Senator from Indiana says, with respect to the alleged complaints against General Lane, that he has searched the Department and can find nothing of the kind. He goes into the curious exposition of the imaginary contest between the Departments for power and patronage, by way of showing that he had found the proper place to make search for papers, if there were any, and that he had found nothing. Where he searched, in the State Department, he could of course find nothing, and he certainly ought to have known it. It was matter that belonged to the Indian bureau of the Home Department, and he had but to go there and find it.

Mr. WHITCOMB. That is the very place to which I did go.

Mr. EWING. I referred to the Senator from Indiana, not now in his seat, (Mr. BRIGHT,) who says that he searched in the Department of State and found nothing. He was truly fortunate, for, if he had found something, perhaps it might have interfered with the beauty and perfection of his speech; especially that part of it in which he gives vent to his virtuous indignation for my unfounded aspersions of the official character of General Lane. The Senator saw fit to say he wished it understood that the statements made by me with respect to those complaints rested on the authority of my assertion alone.

Well, suppose it did rest there; is not the statement of a Senator in his place sufficient authority for a fact within his knowledge? It used to be so when I was a member of this body some years ago. The Senator from Indiana is better able than I am to determine how it is now. But that Senator cannot have his wish; the fact does not rest on the statement of the Senator from Ohio, but is also sustained by a document which I have before me. The Senator demands, however, specifications, and he has a right to them. He requires me to designate what were these complaints, and I will do it. The first charge was that General Lane did not exert himself as he might and ought to have done to separate the Indians from the white population, and to prevent them from camping in the towns, where they became, from their gross habits, offensive to decency. Whether this charge be true or false I know not, but it was vouched by the Delegate from Oregon in two letters, which I now have before me, subject to the inspection of the Senator from Indiana, whenever he chooses to examine them. The first is as follows:

"WASHINGTON, *February* 6, 1850.

"SIR: This morning I had a conversation with Mr. Brown, Commissioner of Indian Affairs, relative to the Indians located in Linn city by Governor Lane, and concerning which I had an interview with you last night. He, like yourself, heartily concurs in their removal from the limits of the town. He said it would be proper that it should be stated in the order to the

Governor that the removal was in no way to affect any title said Indians might have to the lands. To this I very willingly consented. Now, the town there was laid off out of a part of two claims, the Linn city part by Robert Moore, and the Multnoma city part by Hugh Burns. I am aware that the Indians will not be removed unless the order is *peremptory* and *unequivocal*. I have to desire you, therefore, to cause an order to be issued to Joseph Lane, Governor of Oregon Territory, or to his successor in said office, or whoever may be discharging the official duties of Governor and Superintendent of Indian Affairs when said order shall reach the seat of government of said Territory, to cause all Indians, now camping or living within the towns of Linn city or Multnoma city, as laid off in lots by Robert Moore and Hugh Burns, in Oregon Territory, at the Falls of the Willamette river, to be removed outside the limits of said towns, and not to allow the same to return within said limits for the purpose of camping and dwelling.

"I have been thus specific because I believe your order should be so to the letter to ensure obedience. I should have added, provided the order and removal consequent thereon shall in no way affect any title which said Indians may have to the lands included within the limits of said towns.

"Let me assure you, sir, that such an order will be greeted by the people of said towns or villages with gratitude, and the modesty of our women not a little relieved by its prompt execution.

"I would suggest that your order go as soon as possible, and if you will cause me to be furnished with a duplicate, that I may inform the people, in case the order should not be obeyed, that the Department has desired otherwise, you will oblige me.

"I have the honor to be, sir, with high consideration, yours, truly,

"SAM. R. THURSTON.

"Hon. THOMAS EWING, *Secretary of the Interior*."

The second letter I will not read. It refers to and enforces the same charges.

Now, I wish it understood that I affirm nothing and know nothing of the facts stated in these letters, except that I know they come from the Delegate from Oregon, who is of course entitled to attention and respect in all things which he states touching the interests of the people of that Territory. Whether he represents the case truly or not, I cannot determine, and I assume no responsibility concerning it.

The next charge is, that General Lane not only did not prevent the British Hudson Bay Company from keeping up trading establishments in the Indian territory of the United States in Oregon, but that he encouraged, and patronized, and maintained them there, to the injury of the rights of American citizens. One paper goes further, and says that he purchased, or directed to be purchased, from the Hudson's Bay Company, blankets in considerable quantity, and then suffered that company to distribute them as presents from themselves to the Indians. I cannot say that this is true; but it is the charge, presented by the Delegate from Oregon, certified to and sustained by the Chief Justice of Oregon, both Democrats, and both supposed to be responsible men. These charges come, then, as I said, from authentic and reliable sources.

Mr. DODGE, of Iowa. Will the Senator from Ohio allow me to make an inquiry?

Mr. Ewing. Yes, sir, I yield to an inquiry.

Mr. Dodge. Were these charges, which the Senator asserts were made, before the removal of General Lane?

Mr. Ewing. They were not, and I did not say they were—nothing of that kind. Being called on suddenly, the other day, touching the official conduct of General Lane, I threw out my impressions at the moment as to what had been objected against him, without stating the time when the charges were made. These charges, however, were made orally long before the papers which I have produced bear date; for I had frequent conversations with the Delegate on the subject, and he pressed the alleged grievances of his people strongly upon me long before he presented them in writing. I produce them now only to sustain my own statement of fact, indirectly questioned by the Senator from Indiana, (Mr. Bright;) not to sustain the removal of Governor Lane, which, as I find on examination, rests on other and very different grounds.

It is but fair that I should say that the specifications in the last charge, namely, that the blankets purchased of the Hudson's Bay Company for the Indians were distributed by the servants of that company as presents from them, upon investigation, proves to be unfounded. I have looked at the evidence taken upon the spot, which disproves it. But the *general charge* which I have referred to above is sustained—namely, that he suffered the Hudson's Bay Company to trade with the Indians in Oregon; and it is further shown, by Governor Lane's own vouchers, that he bought from houses of that company, at some five or six places in the Territory, sundry articles of merchandise for the Indians. When the new superintendent reached Oregon in September, 1850, he found the Hudson's Bay Company still trading, and claiming a right to trade, there with the Indians, as they pretended, under treaty stipulations. Now, it is clear that the treaty gives them no such right; they are protected by it in their property, but not permitted to become or continue to be Indian traders. They are allowed to navigate the Columbia river and its branches from the 49th degree of latitude to its mouth, and to pass its rapids by the usual portages; but they are not authorized to go beyond that; and no foreigner has a right to enter the Indian territory to trade under any circumstances. No one, not even an American citizen, has a right to do it without a license from the Superintendent of Indian Affairs.

The charge against him of allowing the British Hudson Bay Company to trade in the Indian territory is substantiated; and I think I have said enough to satisfy the Senator from Indiana himself, when he shall read my remarks, and the documents which I have quoted, that he could not possibly be gratified in his very reasonable wish that the public should understand that this charge rested upon my statement alone. I submit whether it is not sustained by quite as good vouchers as I gave the Senate to understand I had for it.

I will now refer, Mr. President, to another branch of the subject. The other day, when this resolution was under discussion, my friend from North Carolina (Mr. Mangum) said he had an impression on his mind, derived from the public prints, that not only was there a publication made by General Lane which reflected upon General Taylor's personal honor, but which went to the extent of an impeachment of his veracity as a man; and that, if so, Governor Lane ought to have been removed. To these remarks the Senator from Indiana, not now in his place, (Mr. Bright,) replied:

"I did not misunderstand the honorable Senator from North Carolina. I did not say that he asserted that Gen. Lane had made such publication, or that he uttered such declaration; but hypothetically, that if Gen. Lane had done so he ought to have been removed. I concur with him in that opinion, unless he stated the truth."

Now, on full proof being made, first, that Gen. Lane made a publication impeaching the veracity of Gen. Taylor; and, secondly, that such publication was not true, the Senator from Indiana, instead of condemning, joins with us in sustaining the removal of Gen. Lane, and will agree that his removal was not "*proscription*" on the part of Gen. Taylor, but the performance of a duty. Those two propositions I will now proceed to establish. I will, as briefly and as hastily as possible, give the facts necessary to sustain them; and, having done so, I shall leave Gen. Lane, and dismiss this branch of the case.

In the first place I am to inquire, did Gen. Lane make a publication which impeached the veracity of Gen. Taylor? I will read a few extracts published during the electioneering contest of 1848, after Gen. Lane was appointed to office, and a few days before he set out for Oregon, which will satisfy every man that he did not only *insinuate* an impeachment of Gen. Taylor's veracity, but that he impeached it directly, and in the grossest terms:

FIRST EXTRACT.

"To the public.—It has become necessary that I should appear before the public and ask its candid attention to a subject of vital importance to Indiana, and to the brave troops which she sent into the field during the war with Mexico. Interested partisans in this State (and I regret that it is so) appear resolved upon disgracing themselves and the State of their nativity or adoption by the publication of glaring falsehoods and statements, wholly unfounded in fact, put forth in the attempt to secure a mere partisan triumph. *I allude to the slanders which, from time to time, have been perpetrated* by different persons, *both in official documents and otherwise*, upon the second Indiana regiment, relative to their conduct in the battle of Buena Vista."

SECOND EXTRACT.

"Gen. Taylor, in his report of that battle, was mistaken as to the facts, and has made statements wholly at variance with them, particularly with regard to the conduct of that regiment. If he had hastened to repair the injury thus inflicted as soon as he became apprized of it, the present statement from myself would not have been necessary. *But, instead of correcting what he has stated, he persists in repeating it in the most offensive manner, and that, too, in the face of facts too numerous and too well authenticated to be denied or evaded.*"

THIRD EXTRACT.

"There are two material facts known to every one upon that field, *known to Gen. Taylor when he made his report,* and which are embodied in my report, which facts Gen. Taylor does not even allude to, to wit: First, that the regiment immediately rallied, and next that they fought all day. Read again those sentences in the above extracts and contrast them. *Gen. Taylor* says *they could not be rallied,* and took no further part in the action, except a handful of men who rallied under the gallant Col. Bowles. *This statement is not true.*"

FOURTH EXTRACT.

"I will give his exact language. Extract from his letter to G. G. Dunn, dated

"'BATON ROUGE, *March* 24, 1848.

"'My confidence in the second regiment, officers and men, was still maintained after the occurrences of the 23d; for I remembered that in all armies the best and most experienced troops have at times been most unaccountably subject and yielded to panic, by no means compromising their reputation for bravery.'

"Extract from his letter to Defrees, dated

"'BATON ROUGE, *March* 3, 1848.

"'In all armies the best and most experienced troops have been at times subject to panics under a murderous fire of an enemy, which are inexplicable. Such, it was most probable, may have been the case at the time in question.'

"*This charge of cowardice, thus repeated again and again,* I KNOW TO BE FALSE, *and so does every man who has carefully and without prejudice examined the case.*

"General Taylor further says that he had not lost his confidence in that regiment, and intended to place them in action the next day. *I let this pass for what it is worth.*

"General Taylor asserts that nothing has transpired since he made his report, nor has any statement been made to him in an official shape, which affects its accuracy.

"*The first of these assertions I have shown to be utterly devoid of truth.*"

I suppose I might be excused from commenting upon these extracts further than to say that they convey very truly the temper and character of the publication. It is from beginning to end a studied and labored attack upon the veracity of Gen. Taylor. In every paragraph which I have quoted there is at least an indirect accusation of falsehood; in three of them the charge is direct. In the first, he charges Gen. Taylor with *slandering* the Indiana militia in an *official document;* for that the first paragraph refers to him is made clear by the second; and Gen. Lane understood well enough that there could be no *slander* in an official paper unless it were maliciously false. In the beginning of the second extract he softens down the phrase, and says that Gen. Taylor "was *mistaken as to the facts, and made a report wholly at variance with them;*" but, as if he repented of the use of a mitigating phrase, and was eager to retract it, he adds, "if he had hastened to repair the injury thus inflicted *as soon as he became apprized of it,* the present statement from myself would not have been necessary. *But, instead of correcting what he had stated, he persists in repeat-*

ing it in the most offensive manner, and that too in the face of facts too numerous and too well authenticated to be denied or evaded."

The amount of this passage is that Gen. Taylor made, *by mistake*, a report doing great injustice to the Indiana regiment; he was mistaken as to the facts, and made a report *wholly at variance with them.* His report was proved to be erroneous by the most indisputable evidence, but he not only refused to correct it, *but persisted in repeating it in the most offensive manner, after he knew it was false;* that is to say, Gen. Taylor repeated a falsehood after he knew it to be false, slandering the reputation of a body of brave men who fought with him at the battle of Buena Vista, and helped him to achieve that crowning act of his military fame. This is the charge—a wilful falsehood to blast the military reputation of these men.

The third extract denies that Gen. Taylor was ever *mistaken* at all, but avers that he made the alleged *false report* knowing it to be false. He says: "There are two material facts known to every one upon the field, *known to Gen. Taylor when he made his report*, first, that the regiment immediately rallied; and, next, that they fought all day." Gen. Taylor says, "*they could not be rallied, and took no further part in the action*, except a handful of men who rallied under the gallant Col. Bowles. "THIS STATEMENT IS NOT TRUE."

This allegation in substance is, that Gen. Taylor, when he made his report, knew that the second Indiana regiment *rallied and fought all day;* that he states in his report that *they could not be rallied, and took no further part in the action.* Reduced to its most brief and direct expression, the charge here is, *that Gen. Taylor stated a falsehood in his report, knowing it to be false* in two important particulars, affecting the military reputation of the second Indiana regiment.

I need adduce no further proof that Gen. Lane not only insinuated, but that he made a direct charge of malicious falsehood against Gen. Taylor. I am ashamed to sum up the substance of this infamous and detestable publication. I would not suffer it to pass my lips for a moment, though I state it only to confute the libel and to confound the libeller, but that I know every one who hears me will, upon the mere statement, instantly pronounce the accusation false.

In the fourth extract it will be observed that Gen. Lane refers to, and in part copies, two letters from Gen. Taylor, both to the same import, in which, speaking of the second Indiana regiment, Gen. Taylor says that his confidence in them was still maintained; and that "in all armies the best and most experienced troops have been at times subject to panics, under a murderous fire of an enemy, which are inexplicable;" and that such, it is most probable, may have been the case with the troops in question.

In commenting upon the expression of continued confidence in these troops by Gen. Taylor, and his apology for what he considered rather their misfortune than fault, Gen. Lane says:

"*This accusation of cowardice, thus repeated again and again*, I KNOW TO BE FALSE."

This quotation of Gen. Taylor's letters, and the comment upon them, shows how little of truth and fairness there is in Gen. Lane's publication. "This *charge of cowardice, thus repeated again and again!*" Why, there is no charge of cowardice, much less a repetition of a charge of cowardice, in the letters copied. What are we to think of a man who will thus deliberately misrepresent a paper that is before him while he writes, and which he knows will be before his readers while they are reading his comments? If his physical be at all equal to his moral courage—if he could face down an *enemy* with as much coolness and resolution as he can face down the *truth*, he must be bold indeed. But he adds in this same extract: "Gen. Taylor asserts that nothing has transpired since he made his report, nor has any statement been made to him in an official shape, which affects its accuracy. *The first of these assertions I have shown to be utterly devoid of truth.*"

I comment no further on these charges; they are full of naked, gross accusations of deliberate and wilful falsehood. I have now only to show that Gen. Lane, in making these accusations, did not tell the truth; or, in other words, that his charge against Gen. Taylor was not true. Having done so, it is admitted in advance that the removal of Gen. Lane was right; nay, more, in the words of the Senator from Indiana, he ought to have been removed.

I will now proceed to the inquiry whether these charges be true or false. Though perhaps it may be well here to say a few words in reply to the Senator from Indiana, (Mr. BRIGHT,) who says it would, in any event, have been magnanimous in Gen. Taylor to have retained Gen. Lane in office—forgetting as President the injury done to him as a man. This is an afterthought. If Gen. Taylor *ought* to have removed him, as the Senator admitted, if the statement of Gen. Lane were proved false, then of course he *ought not* to have retained him in office, and the desired act of magnanimity would have been a breach of official duty. And it would have been a public wrong to keep in office a false man, the author of an insolent and atrocious libel, when there were true men enough, of at least equal capacity, willing to accept the office. It would have been none the more proper because the libel was directed against the President himself. The officer who possesses the pardoning power is no more entitled to pardon the criminal who has forged *his* name, than one who has taken the name of an indifferent person. He might call it magnanimity to do so, but it would be a breach of official duty and an abuse of power. The Senator was right when he said that, if the publication of Gen. Lane was false, he ought to have been removed. I hold him to the admission, and will now proceed to prove it false.

In order to meet this question fairly, and in all the aspects in which it presents itself, I call attention here to that part of Gen. Lane's publication in which he *professes to give* an extract from Gen. Taylor's report of the battle of Buena Vista, and so much of his own report as relates to the conduct of the second Indiana regiment in the same battle. It is as follows:

Extract from General Taylor's report of the battle of Buena Vista, dated Agua Nueva, March 6th, 1847.

"The 2d Indiana and 2d Illinois regiments formed this part of our line, (the left,) the former covering three pieces of light artillery, under the order of Captain O'Brien, Brigadier General Lane being in the immediate command. In order to bring his men within effective range, Gen. Lane ordered the artillery and 2d Indiana regiment forward. The artillery advanced within musket range of a heavy body of Mexican infantry, and served against it with great effect, but without being able to check its advance. The infantry ordered to its support having fallen back in disorder, being exposed, as well as the battery, not only to a severe fire of small arms from the front, but also to a murderous cross-fire of grape and canister from a Mexican battery on the left, Captain O'Brien found it impossible to maintain his position without support, but was only able to withdraw two of his pieces, all the horses and cannoniers of the third piece being killed or disabled. The 2d Indiana regiment, which had fallen back as stated, could not be rallied, and took no further part in the action, except a handful of men under its gallant Colonel, Bowles, who joined the Mississippi regiment and did good service, and those fugitives who at a late period of the day assisted in defending the train and depôt at Buena Vista."

"My own official report of this part of the battle, and of the conduct of the 2d regiment is as follows:

Extract from my own official report of the battle of Buena Vista, dated Buena Vista, February 25th, 1847.

"I immediately put my column in motion, consisting of these eight battalion companies and Lieut. O'Brien's battery of three field pieces, numbering in all about four hundred men, to meet them. The enemy, when they deployed from the ravine and appeared on the ridge, displayed a force of about four thousand infantry, supported by a large body of lancers. The infantry immediately opened a most destructive fire, which was returned by my small command, both infantry and artillery, in a most gallant manner for some time. I soon perceived that I was too far from the enemy for my muskets to take that deadly effect which I desired, and immediately sent my aide-de-camp to Lieut. O'Brien, directing him to place his battery in a more advanced position, with the determination of advancing my whole line. By this movement I should not only be nearer the enemy, but should also bring the company on my extreme left more completely into action, as the brow of a hill impeded their fire. By this time the enemy's fire of musketry and the raking fire of ball and grape shot of the battery posted on my left flank had become terrible, and my infantry instead of advancing, as was INTENDED, I regret to say, retired in some disorder from their position, notwithstanding my own and the severe efforts of my officers to prevent them. About the same time the riflemen and cavalry on the mountain retired to the plain below. The Arkansas cavalry (who had been posted by your orders in my rear, at the foot of the mountain, to act as circumstances might require) also left their position, the whole making a retrograde movement along the plain towards the rear; at the same time one of the Illinois regiments, not under my command, but stationed some distance in the rear on the right of my position, also retired to the rear.

"These troops, the most of them, immediately rallied and fought during the whole day like veterans. A few of them, I regret to say, did not return to the field at all. * * *

"The men under my command actually discharged eighty rounds, and some ninety rounds of cartridges at the 'enemy during the day.' The 2d regiment, under my command, which opened the battle in such gallant style, deserves a passing remark. I shall attempt to make no apology for the retreat, for it was their duty to stand and die until they received orders to retire. But I desire to call your attention to one fact connected with this affair. They remained in their position in line, receiving the fire of three or four thousand infantry, exposed to a most destructive raking fire from the enemy's battery, posted within point blank shot, until they had deliberately discharged twenty rounds of cartridges at the enemy.

"Some excuse may be found for those who retired for a few minutes, and then rallied and fought during the day; but unless they hasten to retrieve their reputation, disgrace must forever hang around the names of those who refused to return; and I regret to say there were a few from nearly every volunteer corps engaged."

"Here is all that is said in relation to the conduct of the 2d Indiana regiment in that battle, either by Gen. Taylor or myself."

The extract from General Taylor's report is set forth truly by General Lane in his publication. In speaking of this part of the battle, General Taylor says: "In order to bring his men within effective range, General Lane ORDERED the artillery and second Indiana regiment forward." In the actual report made by General Lane to General Taylor on the 25th of February, 1847, he says: "My infantry, instead of advancing, as was ORDERED, I regret to say, retired in some disorder." But in the copy given by General Lane in his publication, in which he attacks the veracity of General Taylor, he changes the word, and instead of "*ordered*," the word in his report, he inserts "*intended*," making the passage read, "My infantry, instead of advancing, as was INTENDED, I regret to say, retired," &c. Here General Lane adduces against General Taylor record evidence—the copy of a public document: he certifies to the truth of it, and he copies it falsely. This falsification of the passage is in an important particular. If General Lane did not report that his men were ordered to advance, and General Taylor had reported that they were, it would indeed have been a departure from the truth as it was before him, unless some other officer having command of those troops so reported to him. Now, why this alteration of the record? The answer is easy. It would convict General Taylor, on mere inspection, of a false statement, to the prejudice of the second Indiana regiment. This was not a word which General Lane could have inserted by mistake. His mind had been and was upon the very word. He changed *ordered* for *intended*, in a supplemental report, made long after the report of February 25th, which he pretends to copy, and long after General Taylor had despatched his report to Washington.

This falsification of the report is not in a matter which relates to property. If it had been, and the written paper evidencing the right of a party had been so altered to his injury, it would have been a high crime; but here it amounts to nothing, for it is only the reputation of a victorious General that it is intended to sacrifice. If in a judicial proceeding General Lane had sworn to the truth of this copy of his record, it would have also been a high crime; but as it is only stated upon the veracity of the man, and the honor of the soldier, it is no such thing. I do not know how gentlemen on the other side will characterize it. There was much at stake, no less than the most important office on the face of the earth; and as General Taylor was a candidate, and as his success rested on his fair and honorable fame, which he had earned by a long life in the service of his country, it was important that that fair fame should be, if possible, blasted—at least General Lane appears to have thought so, and acted upon that opinion; and if it could be done by the alteration of a single word in a single record, it would have been a mighty object easily achieved. It was no difficult task—"it was as easy as lying."

Again: General Lane says in his publication, in the extract which I have read to the Senate:

"There are two material facts, known to every one upon that field—*known to Gen. Taylor when he made his report*, and which are embodied in my report—which facts General Taylor does not even allude to, to wit: first, that the regiment immediately rallied; and next, that they fought all day."

Facts embodied in his report, "*that the regiment immediately rallied!*" Now, after a careful examination of that report, I can say that, to my comprehension, there is no such fact embodied in it. It is not there. There is a singularly confused and unintelligible passage in his report, from which I suppose he intended, when he made the publication, to have such statement inferred; but it contains no such thing directly, and admits of no such inference. Here is the passage:

"By this time the enemy's fire of musketry and the raking fire of ball and grape-shot of the battery posted on my left flank had become terrible, and my infantry, instead of advancing, as was ORDERED, I regret to say, retired in some disorder from their position, notwithstanding my own and the severe efforts of my officers to prevent them. About the same time the riflemen and cavalry on the mountain retired to the plain below. The Arkansas cavalry (who had been posted by your orders in my rear, at the foot of the mountain, to act as circumstances might require) also left their position, the whole making a retrograde movement along the plain towards the rear; at the same time the Illinois regiment, not under my command, but stationed some distance in the rear on the right of my position, also retired to the rear. These troops, the most of them, immediately rallied and fought during the whole day like veterans. A few of them, I regret to say, did not return to the field at all."

In this clause, if any where in his report, the statement that the second Indiana regiment immediately rallied must be found; but we look for it in vain. And does any man suppose that if General Lane knew that this regiment rallied and undertook to state it, he would not have told the story so that it could be understood? He tells of their *retreat* in plain terms; could he not tell his commanding general in as plain language that they rallied and fought? He groups together with them in this paragraph the riflemen and cavalry on the mountain—the Arkansas cavalry and the third Illinois regiment—all which he says made a retrograde movement, but most of them immediately rallied and fought all day. That is true enough. The riflemen and cavalry on the mountain rallied and fought; the Arkansas cavalry rallied and fought; so did the Illinois regiment rally and fight—making most of all the troops he had so grouped together; but he does not say in that report that the second Indiana regiment rallied and fought. If he could have said so, he did great injustice to that regiment that he did not say it in an intelligible manner. If he had said in direct terms that most of that regiment rallied immediately, the matter would have been distinctly understood, and justice, whatever that might be, would have been done them on the spot. But I understand from a military man who was on the ground, that the Illinois regiment and the other troops named by General Lane did not retreat at all, but simply changed their position, as ordered by General Wool. That when the Indiana regiment retreated, he directed the other troops to change their position, and form what is called in military phrase the refuse line, to prevent the out-flanking of his troops by the enemy; so that, if my information be right, General Lane was mistaken, and there was really no retreat at all of these troops; they merely took a new position where they were ordered.

Again: General Lane, having presented the above extracts, says, "Here *is all* that is said in relation to the conduct of the second Indiana regiment in that battle, either by General Taylor or myself."

This statement is incorrect. It is not all that General Lane says in relation to the conduct of the second Indiana regiment in that battle. He says yet more concerning them, and what he says further corroborates the report of General Taylor, and the reports of General Wool and Colonel Davis. General Lane does not again speak of it as a regiment, for it had ceased to be such on the field of battle; but he speaks twice of the part of it which, under Colonel Bowles, had joined the Mississippi rifle regiment, and fought bravely. This is the "handful of men" named by General Taylor, the "fragment" named by General Wool, the "small party of the second Indiana regiment" named by Colonel Davis. The extract from General Lane's report as to them is as follows:

"At this critical juncture the Mississippi regiment, under the command of Colonel Davis, arrived on the field, and, being joined by a part of the second Indiana, met the enemy in a most gallant style, and after a severe and bloody engagement, repulsed them with great loss. In the mean time a large body of lancers, six or eight hundred in number, who had passed down along the left towards our rear, made a most desperate charge upon the Arkansas and Kentucky cavalry, with a view of cutting off and plundering the baggage train of the army, which was at a *ranche* near the battle-field.

"This charge was met and resisted most gallantly by those cavalry, aided by about two hundred infantry, who had taken refuge there after they had retired from the field. This repulse discouraged the enemy, and the Mississippi regiment and part of the second Indiana, being joined by the third Indiana regiment, commanded by Colonel James H. Lane, now advanced up towards the foot of the mountain, for the purpose of dislodging the enemy's force stationed there."

I now call the attention of the Senate to so much of the report of General Wool as relates to the second Indiana regiment, by which it will be seen that General Taylor's official report is fully sustained:

"In connexion with this movement, a heavy column of the enemy's infantry and cavalry and battery on the side of the mountain moved against our left, which was held by Brigadier General Lane, with the second Indiana regiment, and Lieutenant O'Brien's section of artillery, by whom the enemy's fire was warmly returned, and, owing to the range, with great effect, by Lieutenant O'Brien's artillery. General Lane, agreeably to my orders, wishing to bring his infantry within striking distance, ordered his line to move forward. This order was duly obeyed by Lieutenant O'Brien. The infantry, however, instead of advancing, retired in disorder, and in spite of the utmost efforts of their general and his officers, left the artillery unsupported, and *fled the field of battle. Some of them were rallied by Colonel Bowles, who, with the fragment, fell in the ranks of the Mississippi riflemen, and during the day did good service with that gallant regiment. I deeply regret to say that most of them did not return to the field, and many of them continued their flight to Saltillo.*"

I would suggest another inquiry, which seems to me to be of much importance in the determination of this question of veracity. It will be seen, by reference to the public document, that General Lane reported to General Wool, his immediate commander, and that General Wool, after receiving that report, made his report to General Taylor. It will be observed, too, that General Wool was upon that part of the field in person, saw the retreat of the second Indiana regiment, and assisted its officers in the attempt to rally them. "Some of them," he says, "were rallied by Colonel Bowles;" he mentions none others that rallied, and deeply regrets *"to say that most of them did not return to the field."* This General Wool said with General Lane's report before him; and not only so, General Lane was on the spot, and in oral as well as written communication with General Wool. He was his next in rank, and it is reasonable to presume that he was with him in his markee, aiding him to make up his report, and no doubt read, at any rate might and ought to have read it, before it was sent to General Taylor. He could not have been ignorant of its contents, so far as it related to the troops under his command. If, then, General Wool misunderstood his report, why did not General Lane correct it on the spot, and cause a true report to reach General Taylor? Why, at least, was not General Wool applied to to make the correction which General Lane desired? And why is not General Wool, instead of General Taylor, denounced by General Lane for making a false report? If General Lane tells the truth, General Wool's report is more injuriously false. General Lane says in his publication:

"*There are two material facts known to every man upon that field,* * * * * to wit, first, *that the second Indiana regiment immediately rallied;* and next, that they fought all day." General Wool says, in his report to General Taylor : "*I deeply regret to say that most of them did not return to the field, and many of them continued their flight to Saltillo.*" Now, if General Lane's publication be not a monstrous perversion of the truth, how happened he to let this report of General Wool go to General Taylor without correction? And how happens it that he has never yet called on General Wool for a correction, never attacked General Wool's statement, but General Taylor's only, which he well knows to be founded on General Wool's ? I can tell you, sir. General Wool was a Democrat, General Taylor a Whig, and a candidate for the Presidency.

I will now present to the Senate the report of Colonel Davis, and would refer, in connexion with it, to the remarks made by him in the Senate yesterday, which also bear strongly on the pending question :

"As we approached the scene of action, horsemen, recognised as our troops, were seen running dispersed and confusedly from the field. And our first view of the line of battle presented the mortifying spectacle of a regiment of infantry flying disorganized from before the enemy. These sights, so well calculated to destroy confidence and dispirit the troops just coming into action, it is my pride and pleasure to believe only nerved the resolution of the regiment I have the honor to command." * * * * *

"With a few honorable exceptions the appeal was unheeded, as were the offers which I am informed were made by our men to give their canteens of water to those who complained of thirst, on condition that they would go back. General Wool was upon the ground, making great efforts to rally the men who had given way.

"It may be proper for me to notice the fact that early in the action Colonel Bowles, of Indiana, with a small party from his regiment, which he stated was all of his men that he could rally, joined us, and expressed a wish to serve with my command. He remained with us throughout the day, and, under all the circumstances, displayed much personal gallantry."

The following is an extract from the report of Colonel Marshall :

"I was closely observing the movements on the mountain, perceiving that matters were reaching extremes with my riflemen, when I observed that *a regiment of Americans were retreating on my right.*"

This is the last we hear, by any official report, of the second Indiana regiment on the field of battle, and all their official papers leave the mass of the regiment in full retreat. Can any man read these extracts from the reports of the officers commanding on the spot, and believe that they were all mistaken in such an important particular ? Is it to be credited that the second Indiana regiment, or one hundred and fifty men of that regiment, could have joined the Mississippi rifle regiment, and yet Colonel Davis not know it even to this day ? But suppose they did return, and no one knew it except General Lane, who did not think it worth while to report the fact, how was General Taylor to know it ? In truth, Mr. President, the pretence is too absurd to be argued seriously. And worse than ridiculous was the attempt of Gen. Lane to get supplemental report from General Taylor, founded on a newspaper publication, contradicting the mass of consistent official evidence which I have referred to.

Gen. Taylor did not charge these men with cowardice, as Gen. Lane asserts in his publication; but, on the contrary, declared he had not lost confidence in them, and that he intended to give them a prominent place in the action next day, if the enemy rallied. He viewed their conduct with the eye of an exp - rienced and sagacious General, who had seen much and read much, and who knew that such reverses occur among the bravest veterans, without any one being able to perceive an adequate cause. From the very earliest historic records of the operations of armies, we read of such things frequently among troops, acknowledged to be the bravest and the best. The Greeks and Romans believed it to be the work of their rural deity, *Pan*, the god of the woods and the fields; hence the word *panic*. But there is reason enough for the flight of these men to be shown from the transactions of the day. Their officers were quarrelling among themselves, and the most common instinct of self-preservation would teach the men that their lives were in danger of being sacrificed by the feuds of their officers. Such appears to have been the case from what occurred on the field. Gen. Lane ordered Lieut. O'Brien to move his battery forward; but it comes out at last that he did not inform Col. Bowles of this order, or send any order to him; that he merely "*intended*" Col. Bowles should advance. The consequence was, that when Lieut. O'Brien's battery began to move, neither officers nor men of the second Indiana regiment knew where it was going—they were under a terrible fire, and had a right to suppose the battery was about to be withdrawn from their support. If the men retreated under these circumstances, Gen. Taylor ought not to have lost confidence in *them*, as it appears he did not. But these officers either lost confidence, or never had confidence, in each other. Col. Bowles, when he rallied his "*handful of men*," did not join Gen. Lane, but Col. Davis, in whom he and his men had confidence. And Gen. Lane, long after the battle, accuses Col. Bowles of hiding himself in a ravine. If the men knew the state of feeling among their officers, the wonder is, not that they fought no longer, but that they fought at all under their command.

Gen. Lane's publication is now disposed of—disproved in all its injurious parts by official documents. I apprehend no attempt to sustain his statements. They are utterly indefensible in form and fact. And having established the two propositions with which I set out, namely : 1st. That Gen. Lane made a publication impeaching the veracity of Gen. Taylor; and, 2d, that his publication was false, we have a right to claim the admission of the Senator from Indiana, (Mr. Bright,) that "he ought to have been removed." Every body must be satisfied with the evidence; and Gen. Lane himself must be convinced, for his friends here have forced us to force the conviction upon him, that his attempt to blast the honorable reputation of his brave and generous commander has proved worse than futile

I would be glad, Mr. President, if it were in my power, to anticipate the apology which gentlemen will offer for this man and this publication. I know of none. I have endeavored to look at it on all sides, to see what weak points there may be in my position, but here I can find none—no mitigation, no apology for this most detestable and black-hearted calumny. Gentlemen on the other side must endure it, if they endure it at all—must excuse it, if they excuse it all—upon only one consideration, and that is, that Gen. Lane was fighting on their side in a fierce political contest, and that this was one of their usual weapons of party warfare; that he drew it from the party armory, and wielded it, as far as he was able, with effect. If the shaft fell harmless at the feet of the intended victim, it was not the fault of Gen. Lane; he discharged it with all his force, and the point was well tipped with venom. Let this, then, excuse him, as far as it may, with his own political friends; with us he can have no apology. No words can be too strong to convey the just abhorrence of his detestable falsehood and ingratitude. But I have done with him.

I felt great reluctance to touch this question at all, as it necessarily involves the consideration of individual character and conduct. But I may say, in accordance with the remarks made by the Senator from North Carolina yesterday, that, if this resolution had passed, calling for the causes of removals, and if Gen. Taylor had answered it, he would have given causes for the removals in the leading cases, such as we have been discussing, entirely satisfactory to the minds of all candid men. I do not suppose he would have given reasons in every case, for it would necessarily have occupied much time, involved much expense, and resulted in no practical benefit to the country. The subject of the resolutions were, I believe, little thought of, certainly but little spoken of by him, for he well believed, as did every body else, that there was no serious purpose to pass them. But, had they passed, and had they been answered, it would have been found that Gen. Lane, though one of the most unscrupulous, was not one of the ablest of those engaged in this species of warfare. There were older and better soldiers in the field than he; more matured and better disciplined in these peculiar tactics; trained to the destruction of personal character, as the Thugs of India are trained to the destruction of individual life. Gen. Lane in this was like the classic Bardolph in a kindred department of the fine arts—"he was too open;" "like an unskilful singer, he kept no time" or measure; he had valor, but no discretion. But there were others who managed the business better—old, experienced manufacturers of libels, who worked them off to order, and furnished any kind or quantity for their country customers; and generally, not always, the public offices of the United States, in the various sections of the Union, were the branches of issue from which this false currency was put in circulation.

During the last canvass, and during the existence of Gen. Taylor's administration, slander and defamation, which had been before habitual but measured in their terms, assumed a character of peculiar violence and ferocity. It is no wonder; Gen. Taylor was deeply intrenched in the hearts and affections of the people, and must be dislodged. His character was bold, marked, and decisive, such as commands the admiration of friends and alarms the fears and excites the hatred of enemies. It must therefore be depreciated and destroyed. Hence the full flood-tide of party fury was let loose at once upon him and his administration. It is no wonder; the waves dash fiercely against the bold promontory which breasts the deep sea, while they roll smoothly over the sloping beach, and sink to sleep upon its sands.

I do not say that every officeholder who was removed placed himself in the same situation with Gen. Lane, either in class or degree. Many, however, fall within the same class. There were those who manufactured the false currency, and those who gave it circulation knowing it to be false, or who were reckless of its truth or falsehood. Generally each one who could say or write an offensive or insulting thing, said or wrote it according to his capacity; and those who could do neither, attended to the distribution of the libels newly made and placed in their hands. Some were the presiding officers of political meetings, or the movers of insulting resolutions. Indeed the officeholders formed throughout the United States an organized electioneering corps, paid out of the public Treasury. Talk of proscription in removing from office under circumstances like these! Why, Gen. Taylor, if he respected himself, if he regarded his friends who had staked so much upon his fair fame, could hold neither official nor social intercourse with men whose daily business was thus to slander and vilify him.

It is of course impossible to classify all the cases, and refer them in general terms to their several causes; but I do not know or believe that there was a single removal without evidence to establish a cause or causes, such as I have named, or some other equally cogent.

All the cases in which no sufficient reason could be made out, Gen. Taylor uniformly refused to remove. The Senators from Iowa will recognise one marked case in their State—that of an officer with more patronage in Iowa and Wisconsin than all the rest combined, whom he absolutely refused to remove, much to the dissatisfaction of his friends in that section of the country, because they could not bring home to the officer any abuse of his official station. Whether he committed any or not, I do not know. It was not proved that he did, and Gen. Taylor would not remove him.

The charge of proscription made against the administration of Gen. Taylor is therefore a false charge. He never did carry out the Democratic doctrine of *removal from office for opinion's sake.*

The Senator from Iowa is right in the heavy and indignant censure which he passes upon the man or men, whosoever he was, or whosoever they were, who taught the doctrine "to the victors belong the spoils," and brought its evils upon our country. I agree with him in principle; I urged it here in my place many years ago, not in the same choice figures and phrases, for they had not yet found their way into the Senate chamber. But to these I do not object; it were idle to dispute about tastes since we agree in principle, and it is gratifying to find that that is the case. The point which he maintains I maintain. It requires but a change of phrase, and a change of names, to make our concurrence complete. In the abstract proposition we agree exactly—namely, that those who brought this evil upon our country owe a heavy responsibility to the nation and to posterity. The Senator from Michigan (Mr. Cass,) does not touch this question. He is too wise; has lived too long, and the past is too fresh in his memory. He rests satisfied with stoutly maintaining his point, from which there is no danger of his being driven, as it lies far out of the range of my argument.

The answer to the resolutions, as amended by the Senator from Kentucky, carrying the inquiry back to 1825, will show those of us who do not remember, who it was that planted the tree from which you now reap such bitter fruit. In the canvass of 1824 there were four candidates for the Presidency. Neither of them was elected by the people, and Mr. Adams came in by a vote of the House of Representatives. Much more than half the people, and, as I well believe, more than half the officeholders in the United States, opposed his election. When he became President, did he remove any one from office because he opposed him? Not a man! In the terrible contest of 1828, a very large proportion of the officeholders, probably a full half, opposed the re-election of Mr. Adams, and supported the rival candidate; even for this, as far as I can ascertain from the records of the times, he did not remove a man! In his whole four years there were but four removals which involved the action of the Senate.

Then, until the commencement of Gen. Jackson's Administration, in 1829, there had been no proscription; there were no wrongs to be righted—no injuries to be avenged. The fierce passions of men had not yet become enlisted in these contests, and justice did not require the interposition of the avenger. But in 1829 the full blown mischief burst suddenly upon us in all its intensity. The Government was likened to a city taken by storm, and delivered over to pillage. The detestable doctrine, "*to the victors belong the spoils,*" was openly avowed, and, as far as my knowledge extended, was fully and effectively acted on. The policy and purpose of the triumphant party was promulgated through the country by words and signs. It was a *general sweep* of all the officers. In 1666 the Dutch Admiral De Ruyter sailed with a broom at his mast-head, and over his flag, to show that he intended to sweep the British navy and commerce from the ocean. So for years over our whole broad land the *broom* appeared at the top of each hickory pole over the flag of the Union—a pregnant sign, indicative of the feeling industriously excited and sedulously cherished. The admonition of the mad Timon to Alcibiades,

"Let not thy sword skip one,"

was universally and unconditionally regarded. There was large destruction of the just hopes of men and the dependence of families.

Before 1829 there were contests for office—there was victory and there was defeat—but they touched the higher objects of ambition only; the love of distinction and power, not the living of the official drudge, the wages of whose labor was the support of his family. But at that time the appropriation of the *spoils*, a term descriptive as it was new and alarming, included every thing. I remember well the opening of the fearful drama, and the sad impressions which rested on my mind in witnessing its then present, and looking to its future, consequences. I felt that it was the origin of stupendous evils to my country, and looked upon it as I would have looked upon a plague-spot on the breast of a venerated parent. And it *was* a new era in our history, when a malignant poison was infused into the body politic which no physician has yet been found potent to eradicate. The poisoned arrow is still there, and can be effectually extracted by those only who infixed it. But from that quarter there is at present but little hope. Do I err in supposing that, give you power, or let you seize power this day, the proscription of past years would be at once renewed in all its intensity? I may be mistaken, and hope I am. If these resolutions were offered and speeches upon them made in sincerity and truth, with a view to put down a vicious and false principle of action, and not merely to avert public indignation from the real authors of the mischief, and point it against others, a change is indeed going on where it may produce the happiest effects. From 1829, year after year, argument was exhausted on this subject, but it was felt to be idle. We talked to the whirlwind, to the tornado. You were deaf as the sea and blind as its rocks. *Now* your ears and eyes are opened, and your tongues unloosed. The prospects of reform are therefore brightening. Our Democratic brethren begin to see, and I trust that time and close observation will show them more distinctly, the practical working of their own favorite system; and practical lessons can alone convince them of the monstrous abuse which they have originated and continued. Mercury himself, though the god of eloquence, could not by mere language have impressed the Gorgon with a perception of her horrors; but she saw them reflected by the shield of Perseus, and, like her beholders, was turned to stone. And if Gen. Taylor did all he has been accused of doing in the way of proscription—if he removed merely for opinion's sake—he only held up the shield, which, by a faint reflection, has shown to modern Democracy the coil of snakes in her own locks. But he did not this. It was characteristic of that excellent man—generous and kind as he was brave—that he often forgot his own wrongs and those of his friends, in sympathy for the afflictions of his enemies and detractors. He did not, but I do not say that he ought not to have meted to you the same measure which you gave to others when the power was yours. Now, we all know that for twenty years, from 1829 to 1849, with the exception of a few short months, the Whigs, composing one-half the nation, equal certainly to the other half in intelligence, in patriotism, in devotion to our glorious Union, and in capacity to serve it, were proscribed for opinion's sake, and denied to that extent the political rights of American citizens. No matter how great his capacity, how high his favor, or how urgent his necessities, the disqualification was absolute of every Whig, and even of every Democrat who would not avow himself such according to the newest platform. All right to office, or hope of office, was denied to those who would not swear—not exactly to the thirty-nine articles—but to the resolutions of the last nominating convention, or to the last exposition of political opinion by the successful candidate. If the Democracy had prevailed in the election of 1848, the test of competency would have been the newest exposition of the Nicholson letter.

Amid all their mutations in other particulars, in this one article of their political faith—the doctrine of the "*spoils*"—the Democracy never changed or wavered so long as they held the power. They were fixed in their opinions, firm in their purpose, and stern in its execution; their march was always onward—

> "Like to the Pontic sea,
> Whose icy current and compulsive course,
> Knows no retiring ebb,"

without change in their object or faltering in its pursuit.

But in 1849 the scene was changed. The proscribed party, the glorious Whig party, who for twenty long years had borne, but never bowed, to the insolence of power, triumphed, and the man of their choice was in the Presidential chair. Now, in this state of things, if the case presented by the mover of these resolutions had in fact occurred; if all the Democrats in office had been removed, and Whigs appointed in their stead, what right would you have to complain? It were but "even handed justice," which "commends the ingredients of your poisoned chalice to your own lips." And the wailing and accusations of the party, now they have lost some of the spoils, appear to me as mean-spirited as false. When in the full possession of power, they were

> "Lion-mettled, bold, and took no care
> Who chafed."

This change of bearing under a reverse of fortune indicates a want of consistency in qualities, a feebleness of temper seldom found among men whose trade is spoliation, or among the predatory part of the animal world. The stern to inflict are generally firm to endure. If the offices be spoils, as democratic language and usages have pronounced them, and we spoil the spoilers, they should meet their reverse like men, and not ask us and ask the nation to weep with them because the spoils which they seized are rent from them in their turn.

The Senator from Indiana (Mr. Bright) "wears his rue with a difference." His distress arises from the alleged fact that Gen. Taylor gave pledges and has violated them. Pledges to whom? To those men whose merits we have been discussing, or to them and their fellow laborers in the work of defamation? To the twenty or thirty thousand office holders organized as an electioneering corps, of whom, sad to tell! three or four thousand most active, most capable, and most vociferous gentlemen were removed the very first year of Gen. Taylor's Administration—cut off in the midst of their patriotic labors, while earnestly engaged in the diffusion of this species of useful knowledge? If it were true that Gen. Taylor made such pledges to them, was there any corresponding equivalent on their part, making a pact which was binding either in morals or in law? Would they or could they have defamed him more, uttered more or baser falsehoods against him, if they had been told expressly that every man of them was to be turned out on the day that Gen. Taylor should take his oath of office at the Capitol? But the case pretended does not exist. He turned no man out of office who was protected by the terms of any pledge which he ever made. The complaint is therefore as unfounded as it is pitiful.

But the party who have brought this great evil on the country, and who now feel and seem to deplore it, can apply the remedy, if they ever regain power, as they probably will at some future day, which I trust in God will be far distant! When in the tide of time that day shall come, if it ever do come, say at the end of another cycle of twenty years; when the Whigs shall have indemnified themselves fully by the enjoyment of official honor and official emolument in their turn for twenty years; and when you shall have drunk to its dregs the bitter cup which you so long held to their lips; then, when

> "The wheel is come full circle,"

and you are again in power, remember to retain the abhorrence which you now feel for "*proscription*;" forget your ancient love of place and power; forego, once for all, the spoils of victory, and join with the Senator from North Carolina; and in that state of things the whole Whig party will join with him and you, and form one great Union party—a party which will abhor detraction, which will detest the libeller and slanderer, and the members of which shall spurn offices, or hold them only because the people have need of their services —a party which shall consider men as nothing, the Union as every thing. When the Democracy shall bring into power a temper and a purpose such as this, then, and not till then, will the evil which they have brought upon the nation be removed.

www.ingramcontent.com/pod-product-compliance
Lightning Source LLC
LaVergne TN
LVHW011133110826
845150LV00008B/2323

* 9 7 8 1 4 1 8 1 9 4 8 3 3 *